THE MAN WHO MURDERED A QUARTER OF THE WORLD'S POPULATION

Factual: It Did Happen

IRA J-IRA

authorHOUSE®

AuthorHouse™ UK
1663 Liberty Drive
Bloomington, IN 47403 USA
www.authorhouse.co.uk
Phone: 0800.197.4150

Scripture quotations marked KJV are from the Holy Bible, King James Version (Authorized Version), first published in 1611. Quoted from the KJV Classic Reference Bible, copyright ©1983 by The <u>Zondervan</u> *Corporation.*

Published by AuthorHouse 12/14/2016

ISBN: 978-1-5246-6731-3 (sc)
ISBN: 978-1-5246-6732-0 (hc)
ISBN: 978-1-5246-6730-6 (e)

Print information available on the last page.

Any people depicted in stock imagery provided by Thinkstock are models, and such images are being used for illustrative purposes only. Certain stock imagery © Thinkstock.

This book is printed on acid-free paper.

CONTENTS

ABOUT THE BOOK

I have written this book as a result of a men's group discussion on *The Power of One*, centered on the Sudanese lady Meriam Ibrahim, who was sentenced to death for her Christian beliefs and was made to give birth while chained up by her legs in prison. Her story was broadcast around the world. Many great men were mentioned as having great power and changed situations. When it was my turn to speak, I mentioned this man who'd murdered a quarter of the world's population. The place went very quiet. After about twenty seconds, I explained that they have probably met him by reading about him, or they heard someone talked about him but did not realize that this man had murdered a quarter of the world population. When they saw it, the place was in an uproar, and there was great laughter. I had to beg them to settle down in order for me to finish my talk.

CHAPTER ONE

It began like this

Who is the man who murdered a quarter of the world's population? He is the man everyone should know, but most don't. He is a man of few words, and that is probably why he is not readily recognized by the masses. Very few realize that this man has done this horrible deed. He has been kept hidden in the blaring light of history. You have probably met him sometime in the past—perhaps many times. Perhaps it was while you were riding on the bus or train, and you saw or heard someone talking or reading about him. Or maybe you were sitting in church and listening to a sermon being preached, and you met him. Some believe that he might still be alive and protected by a government that admires his creative ability to destroy; that could be any government in the world. It is a well-known fact that human beings admire the bad guy. Even though he might be feared by most people, he might still have a strong following of admirers. One of the things known about this man is that he was brought up as a farmer.

His family was quite dysfunctional. Although it is not necessarily common in this modern time that we are living in, it was customary for the man to be regarded as the head of the house not long ago. His responsibility was to provide not only for his family's necessities such as food, clothing, and shelter but also for protection against anything that dared to threaten or harm them in any way. He was the watchman, the protector, the provider. Yes, like all bad guys, he also had some good within him, but you have to look hard to notice it. For instance, after he committed that genocide and was cast out of his society, he became fearful and did not want to lose the comfort of his family and friends. Yes, he had human weaknesses and fears deep within him.

His mother was very beautiful, but she had one basic fault that set this man on his course to become the only person in history to be known as the man who murdered a quarter of the world's population. She was provided with a most beautiful home and all she could ever wish for at her disposal. She did not have to struggle through the nine-to-five traffic madness. She did not have to ask or beg for anything, because her house was well stocked. Her husband brought home the foods that gave good health to the eater and disregarded those that would cause injury—or, worse, kill them. Before he left home to attend his various duties on his farm, tending the fruit and various animals in his care, knowing of her tendency to please herself, he instructed her as to what should not be eaten and what could.

They lived on a farm that was given to them by a rich, benevolent owner. He owned an estate so vast that as far as the eyes could see, all was his. He told them that as long as they looked after their farm and took good care of it, he would let them live there as if they owned it. He loved them and gave them good advice. He knew well the seasons for sowing and reaping, what could be sown in winter, what could be sown in spring, and what could be sown in summer and autumn. He instructed them on the best way to look after this farm. They were accountable to him. He was the owner, and besides having perfect knowledge of the growing seasons, he had perfect knowledge of what should be eaten and what should not. They would want for nothing if his instructions were carried out. They were also told that they could live in this farm for free as long as they followed his instructions and kept out all that would cause harm. Not only that, but if they practiced good husbandry of the farm and taught their children how to take care of their farm, he would give them the whole estate as an inheritance! Their farm was a section of the estate, situated on the eastern side of his estate, with a gentle, flowing stream within it.

But she had that one great fault: she was self-willed. She liked to have her own way, which naturally led to her disobeying the head of the house, her husband. His farm was laden with an abundance of life-giving, healthy foods, but she chanced upon a fruit that looked appetizing but was poisonous. She ate of this poisonous fruit. It tasted sweet, and there was no noticeable immediate negative effect.

While he was very busy attending to his various activities on the farm, she prepared a dish that was very bad for them. But with the beauty of the ingredients and the aroma, she felt that her husband would be foolish and insensitive and would not know what he was missing out on if he objected. This was good food! He came home and was overcome by her praise of this dish. He was seduced by her charm, and he ate it. But as soon as he took a very small portion of that dish that contained one of the poisonous fruits, they both became violently sick. He suddenly realized that the owner of the farm had told them the consequences of not following his instructions. He then remembered the owner said if they ate the poisonous fruit, the owner would become displeased. This would cause the relationship with them to be broken. He and his wife would lose all the privileges that they had enjoyed.

The authority, the estate owner, learnt of their disobedience and subsequently turned them out of that rich and fruitful farm. Perhaps they had never heard the saying of the wise, "Take fast hold of instruction: let her not go: keep her; for she is thy life."

In time, they had two sons, and they had different attitudes toward them. Of course they loved them both. The eldest son was especially loved by his mother. His attitude about life was very much like that of his mother; he was self-willed and took pleasure in living outside the law. His younger brother, however, was favored and loved by his father, and he was honored by the authority because he was very caring to those with whom he came into contact. He presented to the authority a suitable offering that was desired from him; this was a form of worship to the authority.

His elder brother, however, did not offer the authority what was required of him; what he offered was dirty and unclean. This was a sort of kick in the teeth to the authority, and because of this, the elder brother was rejected by the authority. He lost all the privileges that were the right of the firstborn son, and they were transferred to the second son. He became very jealous and hateful toward his younger brother, and from that moment, he started to plan his younger brother's downfall.

It wasn't very long after that this man, filled with hate and jealousy, set about creating the world's first weapon of mass destruction. He thought that he must first eliminate his brother. This made him the world leader who, although not liked by his people, was at least feared. He turned against everyone, and everyone turned against him. He is the biggest mass murderer that the world has ever known. He killed a greater proportion of the world than World War I, in which it was estimated those killed and injured to be between thirty-eight and fifty million. Like the man who murdered a quarter of the world's population, World War I also started with the murder of one man. In World War II, the number of dead and wounded was estimated to be between fifty and eighty million. It also was started by one man, someone who thought his race was superior to all others and set about conquering first his neighbors and then the world. Thankfully, he was stopped.

One would be surprised to know that after all the carnage of World War I, the world plunged itself into yet another war. It is as if love, peace, harmony, and life itself are totally foreign to the human nature, and hate, jealousy, strife, and evils of every kind are preferable qualities. Instead of people caring for one another, World War II reared its ugly head. The result was more blood spilled on the ground. And the ground, not wanting this, cried out, "Stop! I am choking and drowning in the blood of your madness. You are hurting me." But these children of the man who murdered a quarter of the world's population seem unable or unwilling to change their destructive course.

Thus, the earth is having convulsions in the form of great destructive earthquakes that send strong buildings tumbling to the ground like packs of cards; volcanic eruptions, with the earth belching out rivers of molten lava fire and sulfur; tsunamis that send out destructive waves of the sea, sweeping away all that are in their paths; droughts that leave the land parched and dry as the rain refuses to saturate the land, making many go hungry because food becomes scarce when the land cannot produce; and floods, in which many lose their lives and productive farmland and properties as a result of these floods. In addition, hurricanes bring down strong and mighty edifices, especially when combined with heavy rain and strong winds. Fires, whether started spontaneously by human carelessness or through criminal behavior, destroy homes, vegetation, properties, and human lives. There are many other tragic events happening, that is the earth shouting and crying out in pain that it is being choked and is drowning by having all the blood of dead people being forced down its belly. The earth, which has supported humans and has given seeds to the sower and bread to the eater, is now being polluted by blood.

CHAPTER TWO

The mother's love?

This man's mother, who was the most beautiful woman in the world, did not foresee that the boy, about whom she claimed "I have gotten a man from the Lord," would soon realize that he would, on reaching manhood, cause so much pain and anguish in the world—so much so that it was said the blood that he spilled cried out, left a continuous pain in the earth, and has been continuous in its crying as the recipient of the blood spilled by murder. It is crying out even more so now, it seems that everybody wants to rule the world in which he lives locally; some want to rule on a global scale. The effects of the murder that occurred then are still being felt by the combatants' children now. How? Through hate and mistrusts, economic wars, trade barriers, racial hatred, trade embargoes, and military conflicts. The way to love and peace is not known to them; it seems that they have never heard the words of the ancient:

"Train up a child in the (peaceful) way he (she) should go, and when he (she) is old he (she) would not depart from it." Peace and security are the very things that these children say they are striving to achieve, yet they sow the seeds of hatred and strife, and they reap what they have sown no matter what they say at their negotiating tables and their peace summits.

In proportion, this man has killed more than his children. The world celebrates the world wars that killed millions, and people have wounded even more, yet the world is quite ignorant of this man who murdered a quarter of the world's population! The nuclear bomb was dropped over Hiroshima, and it is estimated over 130,000 were killed, most instantly; thousands more were traumatized with life-threatening injuries and cancers. Another nuclear bomb was dropped over Nagasaki, where it is reported that more than 69,000 were killed instantly, and thousands more suffered and were traumatized. There was also the Arab Spring, which started by one man setting himself on fire, which was the spark that lit the fuse that set the Middle East on fire.

Thousands lost their lives, their properties, their livelihoods, driven from their familiar surroundings through fear of genocide, atrocities, and mass murders that were taking place. That fire is still burning brightly right now. Many have fled and are still fleeing, seeking refuge in Europe. These heinous acts are well known and recorded on the pages of ancient and recent modern histories in every corner of the globe. Yes, they are well known—yet no one recognized him, the man who murdered a quarter of the world's population! No one celebrates him; not even his own children want to be associated with him. He is kept on the open pages of history, yet people haven't realized that they have met him. No one realized that this man sets in motion the quest to develop the invention of the most heinous weapons that would kill as many of his own children, their own brothers, as possible. Yet his act is written on the pages of an open book. How strange!

The children that he begat are spending billions, even trillions of dollars, pounds, and other currencies, trying to invent new ways to kill as many of their own brothers as their father did. Days and nights are spent frantically in pursuit of finding the most effective weapon to rival their father's genius. He used a knife as his murder weapon, but they have succeeded in creating weapons far more destructive and superior than the humble knife. In their quest to rule the world by deadly force and with weapons of mass destruction, there exists intercontinental ballistic nuclear weapons, with fifty times the power as the bomb dropped over Hiroshima.

The authority, being very observant, noticed that this older brother was angry and filled with rage. The Authority said to him, "If you do wrong; should you be rewarded for good?"

The authority reasoned with this man, but he was so set in his own ways, was so spoilt, was so arrogant and rude that he said to the authority, "You are turning me out of the society, away from my family, and now all who see me will kill me. You're turning me into a vagabond and a fugitive on the earth. This punishment is too much for me to bear." He was in effect accusing the authority of acting like an uncaring dictator. Isn't it strange how a person would conclude that the law is unjust when he is judged, found guilty, and sentenced for his unjust and hurtful crime?

His mother doted on him, her firstborn son. She even shouted to the world at his birth, "I have gotten a man from the Lord!" Yes they were very close, and naturally he watched her and learnt whatever there was to be learnt from her, except that he never learned to cook, because his mother did all that. As farmers, they supplied the food like their father, and she cooked it. But there was trouble brewing. He copied her selfishness, and that was where the trouble started; he wanted to rule the world. It was his right to be the ruler, because being the firstborn in the family entitled him to it. He had the right to be ruler of society after his father's rulership came to an end. However, his right to this position was forfeited by his murderous attitude, the judge, the ultimate authority over the society, rejected him from ever wearing the crown.

The man sought for another way. He lost the birthright, and so he thought, "I cannot now be ruler," because he judged that he was unfairly treated by the authority, who was the lawmaker and judge. What better way to regain back that power but through democracy! He sought the votes of the people and was soundly rejected at the ballot because he was despised and rejected by society. His younger brother was now chosen to be ruler of the world instead of him.

After losing the crown that should have been his to his younger brother, anger, rage, and fury welled up in his heart. He thought, "My younger brother must be eliminated." He wanted to rule by any means necessary, so he feigned love and affection toward his brother, but he had designed murder for his own brother because he viewed his brother as a thief, a stumbling block, and a usurper. This ravenous ambition of his grew until it became an unstoppable force that led him to murder his own brother. Yes, Cain murdered his brother Abel, and with that act of murdering his brother, Cain became The Man Who Murdered a Quarter of the World's Population. There were four people recorded to be on the earth at that time: Adam, Eve, Cain, and Abel. With that scenario, when Cain murdered his brother Abel, he literally murdered a quarter of the world's population, and he did it with the world's first weapon of mass destruction: a knife!

The authority heard of his violence, and because he was just and fair, he tried Cain and found him guilty. Cain murdered his own brother and so was cast out and banished from his society by the decree of *the authority*. He was now isolated and lonely, and he felt very cross with *the authority* who'd asked him to leave. Having now gained the disfavor of the community, he railed upon *the authority*, who'd banished him from his home because of his unreasonable and murderous behavior. He showed no remorse for his murderous act, and he did not repent; instead, he showed a defiant attitude to *the authority*; who was a very fair and just one. Had Cain showed some respect and become sorry and repented for what he had done, he might have been forgiven and spared this judgment, but now he had set a course for his children to follow—and follow it they have.

Now feeling the pain of his isolation, he married a woman and had seven sons and three daughters, it is believed. As far it is known, he had a happy marriage. The children lived with him until they reached the age of maturity of twenty-one. Living with their father for so long had an impact on those children. He lived to a ripe old age and taught them the art of manufacturing the weapon that he'd used in murdering his brother. They in turn strived and succeeded in creating newer and more powerful weapons of mass destruction.

Cain lived long enough to see one of his grandsons commit murder on a man who had done him no harm whatsoever, except that this man had said to him, "It is against the law to have more than one wife." The boy had two wives. Feeling that he should not be scolded by someone whom he felt was below his lofty position, he used the weapon that he'd copied from his grandfather and murdered the man. When he realized the significance of what he had done, he lamented the fact that he had killed a man who had done him no harm. The grandfather sucked the sour grape, and even his grandson's teeth were set on edge. He lamented and was therefore aptly called Lamenta, because he lamented and said, "I have killed a man to my hurt." The guilty pain he suffered through that great act caused him to confess to his wives what he had done. Through the burden of guilt and sorrow that laid on his sin-laden heart, by confessing, he sought release from his guilt, his sorrow, and the weight beset him.

It is believed that Cain married his own sister, who produced for him seven sons and three daughters. Eventually they all moved away, established their own paths, and separated themselves to the four corners of the earth. They chose their own way and eventually populated the whole world; even their speech changed so that they could not understand each other, except by a few words and sentences that they remembered from their parents. This inevitably caused mistrust and even fear, because no one knew what advances the others had made in inventing their superior weapons of mass destruction.

Now being separated, they began to fight each other for what they perceived to be their rights to be leaders of the world. They were greedy and hunger for power, and wars were the inevitable outcome.

After Cain's children grew up and got married, they naturally left their parents' home and moved away from that toxic environment. They did not communicate with their parents, except for special occasions such as deaths and marriages. Although the children moved away from their father, the nature of their father remained with them—wherever they went, his demon followed them.

As it turned out, Cain never got the chance to rule the world as he had hoped; his brutish behavior caused many to form an opposition party that operated clandestinely, a covert society that weakened his grip on his brutish regime. He was always striving but never ruled the world as he had set out to do. Yes, Cain was the man who murdered a quarter of the world's population when he brutally murdered his younger brother, Abel, but mercifully he was cast out of his familiar home and society. Ostracized, he was prevented by his new society from shedding more blood. He was recognized as a vagabond and a fugitive on the earth.

Frustrated, he gave up the fight of ever having any hope of ruling the world himself, but he elected one of his sons, Absconder, hoping that he would succeed where he had failed. His son was weak and could not fulfill his father's wishes. Most of his children eventually intermarried and formed themselves into tribes and races, but that same devilish and rebellious nature still displayed in them all; it is a genetic condition. Even when some of his children tried their best to reject that murderous and rebellious inclination in themselves, there still arose that spirit of hate and murder through fear and suspicion, lurking just below the surface.

Absconder was very close to his father, but he did not have that burning desire to rule the world as did his father, who was very disappointed by his lack of enthusiasm to rule the world. Nevertheless, he enjoyed hunting and so developed the bow and arrow with which to hunt. It was a quicker way to kill whatever it was that he was hunting, but he soon realized that he could also use this hunting weapon for fighting the enemy.

They raced to develop more sophisticated weapons of mass destruction, using these weapons to threaten or kill any who dared stand in their way in their quest for the power to rule the world. Their striving continued unabated. The opposition, their own brothers to whom they had now become strangers, were now viewed as enemies and a threat to their security and safety, especially because not only did they speak different languages, but they dressed differently and ate strange foods. Not surprisingly, their inability to relate to each other, even though they were of the same flesh and blood, led to them developing their own genius in acquiring the technical know-how to produce and use weapons of mass destruction.

This man's children spread abroad because of his rebellion in dishonoring and defiance against *the authority. The authority* separated them and changed their language, and because their language was changed and they could not now understand each other, they had to be spread abroad to populate the whole world. They were very religious, and in every corner of the world that they occupied, they took their religion with them.

Nimrod is the name of the leader of the rebellion; he set himself in opposition to the authority. His name is synonymous with hunting and warfare, which he learned from his father Absconder.

With suspicion, fear, and the quest of world power through military and economic might, the stage was set for the world to be in a state of continuous warfare. A priest was always called upon to bless the combatants in their individual conflicts, hoping that their national or individual god would bless their efforts in destroying their own fellow men, their brothers. Indeed, the father sucked the sour grape, and it set the children's teeth on edge.

Cain's children, having grown to be very suspicious of each other, began spying, which played an important part and resulted in assassinations. Each time after they waged their wars, which always led to hundreds, thousands, and even millions of people being slaughtered, they came together to make peace—a truce in reality. But behind each other's backs, they worked frantically to produce more weapons of mass destruction.

This of course is not limited to nuclear weapons, but also includes biological weapons that include anthrax, sarin, and many other nerve gases designed to kill, maim, and destroy other human beings. There is also the psychological war of mind manipulation. The victim of mind manipulation does not even know that he is a victim. He is not aware that he is being manipulated and controlled, acting by the command of a manipulator. He is in effect a slave, and his freedom is a prison, but the walls of his prison are invisible.

Nimrod was the ruler who occupied Babylon and became a formidable hunter and worshiper of idols, some of which he made himself. He worshiped these idols and other gods, and he had a large number of priests so that he could call on the ones who he thought were most suited to the desires that he wanted to be fulfilled. It seemed that having these priests were not enough to satisfy his vanity and beliefs, so he brought into his courts magicians, soothsayers, wise men, astrologers, and fortune tellers. Chief among all those were the Chaldeans, who were the high priests who claimed to have the power to interpret dreams, even of things to come in the distant future.

Babylon was the center of worshiping strange gods. This worshiping of idols and strange gods can be found in virtually every nation under heaven, but some of the original idols and strange gods have had their names modified slightly, and some radically with the passage of time, cultures, and influences that their children learnt and adopted.

CHAPTER THREE

Religion

Look around, and you will see a world that is at war with itself—a world that looks to national clerics and priests, employed in the service of their wars, to bless their soldiers so that their prayers are answered by their respective gods. Their war efforts are blessed by the slaughter of their own brothers! Yes, religion has played a very significant role in the world, in the fight to conquer, dominate, and rule the world by any means necessary—except by true love for each other. It's no wonder that with all those strange gods and differing beliefs, confusion reigns supreme.

Virtually all religions are influenced in some way by the religious beliefs and customs of Babylon, including *Christianity*. Strange as it may seem, all of these religions believe that their gods are the only true way to worship; some would even kill should you dare say anything that they regard as being offensive.

They all pray to their "merciful" gods to show them mercy, yet they pray for the deaths of their own brethren who might believe in a different way of worship. They pray for mercy and blessings for themselves from their gods, and in the same breath they pray that their merciful and benevolent gods show no mercy to others, their own brothers.

There are many religions and religious beliefs. In all religions, there is a legend of a flood, which shows that mankind have a common ancestry. There are those who would deny this, even though the fact speaks loudly.

The religion that is most practiced in the Western world is Christianity. The followers of this religion are called Christians because they supposedly follow the teachings and practice of their leader, who is called Christ. Some of his followers believed him to be the son of God, sent down to earth from heaven by the will of God to suffer for the sins of the whole world. While on earth, he went about doing good: heal the sick, open the eyes of the blind, and miraculously feed hundreds with just five loaves and two little fishes; he even cured lepers by touching them. A woman who had a problem with menstrual sickness walked up behind him stealthily and touched the hem of his garment, and she was instantly made whole of her condition.

His followers have different views of him, however. He declared that he was the son of God, and God himself declared, "This is my beloved Son, in whom I am well pleased." Even the chief apostle, Peter, gave answer to the question, "Who do men say I Am?" Peter is recorded as saying, "Thou art the Christ, the Son of the Living God."

Yet some are still debating his relationship to God! Some say, "Jesus is God." Others say, "He is the third person in the God-head." Still others say, "He is a lesser God." You may have noticed that these beliefs and divisions are so akin to the political parties, all with differing beliefs, and all within the same Christian communion. Many strange customs have been developed with claims of being Christian, but after reading through their books of the *Bible*, one cannot find any such customs or beliefs. Some of these customs are *Santa Claus, sleigh rides, sleigh bells,* chestnuts roasting on an open fire, decorated *Christmas trees* with lights, and more. All these things are celebrated on *December 25,* which is supposedly the date that *Jesus Christ* was born. Great merrymaking takes place, but there's ...

No Room in the Inn!

Christmas comes but once a year.

Let the merriment begin.

Get the whiskey, the rum, the beer.

Let's celebrate, let's dance and cheer.

(Well, it's Christmas!)

But where is this Christ we celebrate?

Why is he not here? None seem to care.

To reign as king, he came to earth.

Yet in the *inn*, he can't get in.

(Well, it's Christmas!)

Why can't he get in the inn, you ask?

Well the *inn* is full; there's no room for him.

The turkey, the drinks, the music, the fare—

There is no room for him in here.

(Well, it's Christmas!)

On Christmas morn, the Christians came

To worship the Christ—or so they claim.

But look around, and you will see

They left him freezing cold in the sanctuary.
(Well, it's Christmas!)

Mindful of the gifts on the Christmas tree,
They raced home to join the festivity.
But take a look at this great mystery:
They invite not the Christ to his own party.
(Well, it's Christmas!)

There is someone at the door;
He knocks, but no one hears.
The merriment the dance, the fare—
No one hears, no one seems to care.
(Well, it's Christmas!)

Make room for the Christ, the king of glory.
Open now, his word obey.
Swing the heart's- door widely open.
Let the king of glory come into *your* inn.
(Now, that's Christmas!)

Everywhere Jesus went, he was doing good! Yet he was
judged by the ruling religious elite of his time, delivered up

to the judicial authorities, condemned, and put to death. The works that he did in public and in private demonstrated to the world that their offerings up to God, whom they had claimed to worship and honor, were nothing more than falsehoods. You can see here the spirit of Cain being manifested. Jesus's teaching and clean, honorable service to God was the right way; their way, like Cain's, was not honorable to God. Jealousy reared its ugly head, and they figuratively knifed him to death so that their jealously guarded positions might be maintained. He stood in their way, and they had to eliminate him by any means necessary, just as Cain did to his own brother Abel.

The qualities of a good leader must start with love for those whom he wants to lead. Their welfare must take center stage; it must not be for self-glorification, but it must be for those he wants to lead. These are the first lessons that anyone who wants to lead must learn, but it is in most cases the last lesson that he learns—if ever he learns it at all. The children of Cain seemed incapable of choosing to do the right thing without it being tarnished by what is wrong.

CHAPTER FOUR

Politics

The push for supremacy has led to the introduction of political parties. One would form a political party, and another would form an opposition party in order to challenge that which is proposed by the other. This system seemed to work in what is called a democracy: a leader is chosen first by the cabinet of the party, and if the party wins an election, he then becomes the prime minister or president.

The idea of democracy is, rule by the people and for the people. At first sight this seems reasonable and fair. The people have the freedom to vote for whomever they wish, and there is great rejoicing in the streets as candidates are declared the winners. But soon after the rejoicing, many began to realize that a lot of what was promised has not been fulfilled. True, there are some who will still support this government, but for the majority, their hopes are dashed, and they have now become disillusioned. The opposition party has now become the party of choice. People have switched, hoping that their new party might become better than those who are now ruling the government (and whom they supported not long ago).

Within these parties are segments called wings. There is a: left wing, a right wing, a center wing, a far left wing, a far right wing, within each party. Herein lies the weakness of this form of government: it has too many wings, and therefore it cannot fly straight. They are in reality parties within the party. There is even a tea party within one of the parties. Within these parties, compromises are always being made not because what the leader proposes is wrong, but because of objections being made by one of the wings who want something other than what is proposed by their own ruling government. Just like a bird with a broken wing, the government must swing to the wing that has the most strength of opinion at the time. With their hopes and wishes being unfulfilled, the party in opposition is not slow to point to the government's weaknesses and failed promises, and it is now being hailed as the party that would set the country on the road to prosperity, freedom, and security. This is the longing of every human being on the planet, but can you see what is happening? The hoped-for savior (party) turns out to be just as unfulfilling as its predecessor.

No sooner has this opposition party becomes elected and begins ruling than the same old pattern emerges: disgruntlement with the now ruling party that the people had just elected to rule them. The people are always ravenously seeking the good that they desire but never seem to grasp hold of; it's an illusion.

One of his descendants decided to create a system in which everyone would be treated equally. All the resources would be shared equally, and there would be no lack in his kingdom. He would rule with good intentions in his heart for the entire populace. His ego told him that whatever he did would be good and right for the people. There was one condition, though: no one must own a business and have more than anyone else, even if this was achieved by his own efforts. This theory was called communism.

As in the democratic system, dissatisfaction rears its ugly head. Some of the people with entrepreneurial flair felt frustrated and trapped by not being able to cut a path for themselves, their families, or even their nation. Representation was made to their ruler, but instead of getting the freedom that they required, less freedom entailed because the people were seen as a threat to the ruling party, to the system, and even to their neighbors. Remember the issue with their father Cain? Instead of freedom to excel, they were sometimes cast into prison for years, sometimes until death. This practice was known as Communism.

When others who had the same aspirations, the same fire and desire to excel, observed the fate of the ones who had that same fire and suffered, people's hearts sank and were quickly changed. The fire that was brightly burning in their hearts was quickly extinguished; they had seen what could be their own fates should they resist the repressive hand of their rulers. But the desire to lift oneself above any obstacle, to be different, to excel, and to contribute for the good of family and friends forced them to go beyond the current barriers. To them the future belonged, no matter the suffering, the pain, the injustices of the regimes, or the naysayers.

For the population of these regimes, with their voices silenced by fear, poverty was usually the condition under which they lived. The entrepreneurial flair that would cause the wealth of their nation to be enhanced was stifled. The regimes were so afraid of their own positions that a number of spies are created, even in local neighborhoods, to spy on neighbors and citizens. So potent was the fear generated by these spying activities that every man's neighbor was believed to be a spy working for the masters of the regimes. This morbid fear generated by these regimes was not hard to understand. With their own citizens now having access to interact with their distant relatives coming to visit for vacationing or for the establishment of business relationships, fear and suspicion became a preoccupation of the regime. Visitors were closely watched and monitored, and their own citizens were often forbidden from travelling.

With the ability of other people (their brethren) now entering their domain by way of international trade and diplomatic relations, their fears were greatly heightened because of the poverty of their own people. They feared that their citizens might see the wealth of others, start a revolution, and realize their own extreme poverty. What was seen as a superior way of life that could never be achieved in their own community, and so the people may become restless by wanting more than their economy could afford. If the people's aspirations could not be met, rebellion could ensue, and the regime's iron hold on the people's minds and bodies could be lost. Fear was the regime's biggest weapon, used by all of Cain's children. With all these mountainous barriers leveled against them, and with those who saw their needs and wanted to make a contribution to their fellow man, is there any surprise that with all these obstacles and pitfalls leveled against them, most citizens became impotent? They were threatened and controlled by fear that sapped their entrepreneurial strength, and they almost gave up the fight.

This fear had teeth: imprisonment and sometimes death awaited should their aspirations become known to the regime. Should a man raise his head above the parapet, he'd suffer in the cage of hopelessness and despair. But there were some who were willing to take the risk with a "come what may" attitude, and they eventually succeeded in breaking the mold, forging ahead by that burning desire, and blazing a trail to make the once unknown a common place. With all this fighting and warring to rule the world, it is no wonder that poverty, sicknesses, disease, homelessness, and destitution was rampant among Cain's children.

Military wars and strife have left the poor and helpless crying out for help with no means of fending for themselves. War has led to homes being destroyed, and farmlands cannot be farmed because the land is mined with shells or poisoned with chemicals; unused or destroyed military hardware litters the land. As a result, many go hungry, and their bodies are weakened by hunger; diseases then take their deadly toll. The results of all these conditions is that the poor begin to fight amongst each other. Like fish in a river that is being depleted of the life-sustaining water on which they depend, they are crushed from without, and they are crushed from within. Crime now shows its ravenous head among these destitute ones: robbery from neighbors and friends have become commonplace, and people are defenseless. They are afraid and become prisoners in their own homes—but who cares? Certainly not the rich and powerful of the governments, despite all their protestations of caring for the poor and needy.

These governments—the rich and powerful, the manipulators who are seeking nothing but power, fame, and fortune—care very little about the man in the street. People are destitute, they are trapped, they are crushed and caged, and their bodies are thrown into the sea or fast-flowing rivers like dead dogs.

Have you seen them? Some even kill children, remove organs, and sell them to heartless and corrupt people, the highest bidders! People live at the expense of murdered innocents, and they themselves are still going to die anyway.

Cain and his brother Seth's children occupy every island and continent. Populated by different tribes and races, the children now invent for themselves justifiable reasons (or so it seems to them) to hate their brothers, who seems different by shades of color, wealth, military might, economic power, and technical skills. He who has the most skills, especially military and economic, dominates and subjugates others with military threats or by the use embargoes. Rulers don't care how many are made to suffer, go hungry, and die by this action. Cain and

Seth's children are in possession of two powers, military and economic, and they usually boast how much they are feared, riding roughshod over those who do not have the same might.

There is a gaping hole within the democratic system. The poorer people are always left behind, whereas the rich, the academic, and the so-called upper classes get richer by the day—usually by robbery, thievery, and tax evasion, their wealth hidden away in some foreign country, far away from the very ones who should benefit from some of their wealth. Yes, the poor of the world suffer because of the ravenous greed of rich, powerful nations and governments, with no thought of those who find it difficult to rise. The powerful deliberately push down these poor sick and helpless ones. Many do not know this, and most don't want to know about it.

Cain's children display the same attitude and cunning craftiness as their father. It was while he and his brother were conversing in the field that he turned and slew his brother; it was summer while they were reaping and harvesting the bounty that their land had produced. Cain started an argument with Abel, accusing him of stealing what Cain thought was his: rule of the world. Whilst at the negotiation table in peace talks, when papers are being signed as a token in normality among nations, at that the same time countries are each preparing to outdo, to dominate and kill each other with either a political or economic knife hidden behind their diplomatic backs.

The rest of the family were some miles away. It was a very large farm, so they had no idea what was taking place, and while they were occupied; Cain struck with such sustained ferocity that in no time at all, his brother was dead. Cain murdered his younger brother Abel at the time of harvest. The family was in such great disarray that they forgot to accurately record the date when Cain struck, because at the time of harvest, when their farms yielded an abundance, everyone tended to get over excited and drunk in the process. They were happy because their farm had yielded the longed-for harvest of abundance for which they had toiled to achieve. It was at such a time in the history of the world when murder was unknown among neighbors, much less among one's own family. It was not thought necessary to legislate on such a matter. It was such a heinous crime that he was chased out from his family so that he might not further corrupt the farm, and was chased out by the authority.

How did Cain do it? He was very angry with his brother, but Cain did not let his wrath show. His younger brother was ignorant of the condition of his elder brother's heart and did not take any defensive precautions. It is said, "The heart of man is very deceitful who can know it." They talked together as normal, and everything seems to be as it should. Abel was living by an old maxim: "How pleasant it is for brothers to live together in unity." But unity was the last thing on Cain's mind, as it is in the world today.

Cain began by discussing with his younger brother the best way to rule the world. His idea was that heavy burdens should be placed on those he ruled. He'd whip them into shape and tax them till they squirmed. That was his opinion of good governance. Abel asked him, "Well, what about love?"

Cain said, "Brother, you are just too soft. That is your problem. What's love got to do with it?"

CHAPTER FIVE

Cain's offering rejected

They had presented their offerings to be judged. The authority pronounced that Cain's offering was disrespectful and unworthy of being presented, because he did not bring a live animal as he was supposed to have done. The authority had no respect for his offering, so Cain went away with great anger in his heart. Abel brought his offering to be judged, and it was a young beautiful lamb. There was no blemish on this lamb, and the authority was overwhelmed with this man's offering and said how pleased he was. While they were in the field, talking together, Cain took a sharp knife, walked up behind Abel, and slew his younger brother. The authority, being wisdom itself and full of knowledge, knew that something was wrong. He also knew what the wrongdoing was because he could smell blood coming from the field. Because the authority could not see Abel, he asked Cain, "Where is your younger brother, Abel?"

Cain shouted back to the authority, "He is his own man. He is of age and can do what he wants and go where he wants. I don't know what has happened to him. I am not responsible for him." The authority was full of wisdom and knowledge, and he knew what was wrong and banished Cain from his community, hoping that others might not become contaminated from the crime.

This might seem a little repetitive, but it is for a reason. I am sure that you can observe the spirit of Cain being manifested in so many different ways; it is impossible to miss a lot of them. The rich man has wealth in abundance, which gives him a sort of ruler-ship status—but he tends to strangle his own brother for the little that he has. He wants to rule by brute force, sharpen his knife, and take his weapon with him to fellowship meetings. While the innocent is unaware of the man's wicked heart, out comes the knife, which is plunged deep into his brother's back.

It should not be forgotten that the bringing of the different offering was in effect a religious way of honoring the supreme ruler, the authority. He calls the shots, and they were living on his farm, which naturally gives him the right to make the rules, set laws and ordinances, and set the bounds within which those laws, rules, and ordinances should operate. At least he was thinking of their safety peace and happiness, because he has no need to fight to rule; all belongs to him, and he wants those who inhabit his farm to have the same pure heart of love that he has, showing it to each other.

Train up a child in the way he (she) should go, and when he (she) is old, he (she) will not depart from it. Had Cain's mother not gloated over this boy—she wrongfully shouted, "I got a man from the authority"—things might have ended differently. Instead of the joy that should have been experienced, pain and sorrow now filled their hearts, and they suffered due to the murderer Cain.

It is sad to observe that instead of getting better, the children of Cain and Seth display the same spirit of arrogance and pride. It's a spirit that says, "I want to rule by any means necessary." It's the spirit of "I want," never the spirit of "we want, I love, I care, and I want to help and make a difference." Cain became dictatorial and self-willed, and he showed no respect and gave no honor to the authority. It was a case of true worship and working by the laws and good favor of the authority, who incidentally was the owner of the farm on which they lived. Cain was just a tenant but had freedom of choice. The authority cordoned off a section of his farm that had become contaminated by the disobedience of this man's father before him. Because of the disobedience of Cain, the whole of the authority's farm was even more polluted.

Take a look around the world. It would be impossible for you not to see and hear that in the whole world, wherever this man's children came to dwell, blood cried out from the ground from this man's children murdering one another. The word "murder" has been sanitized so that it is now called "war," but whatever it is named, it is still brother killing brother, and it is still the hunger that is in the brother's heart: "I want to rule the world, whether that world be a village, a country, or the world." Of course, you have noticed that it is those most lacking the necessary qualities of true love and caring who are most likely to be elected to rule over their little worlds—but not the world. That ruler-ship is reserved for the one who has the necessary qualities of love and compassion flowing like a river, like the sun giving warmth to all.

It has been reported that Cain has been spotted. The report has been circulated that he is in China. Others say he is in the Himalayas. But if he was hiding in China, he would have been apprehended long ago because the Chinese features are very distinctive, and hiding there would be impossible. Was he spotted hiding in the Himalayas? This man was not known for climbing, and he does not have a head for heights; neither does he like the cold because he did not get accustomed to living out in the freezing cold. They have probably seen a Yeti. The problem is that genetically, some of his children could easily be mistaken for him because they act just like him. He murdered a quarter of the world's population, and it seems that there are many who are trying to do the same. It must not be forgotten that he murdered his own brother, and some of his children are trying desperately to emulate their father.

The authority's advice was, "If you see this man, do not approach him. This man is dangerous." The authority lives by justice, is supreme in his judgments, and gives a warning that this man must not be approached under any circumstances; he has even put a mark on him. Cain would stop at nothing to escape the justice he so rightly deserved. He was like a kung-fu expert: he looked very calm and nonaggressive. But don't be fooled, because he could wipe out a city with his skills.

Because he had committed this crime and was despised by the majority and the authority, he became resentful and suspicious of everyone. Therefore he had a tendency not to wait for answers before he struck—and when he did strike, it was deadly. Take heed to the authority's advice and do not approach this man. The authority even put a mark on him, so be aware and stand clear, if you know what's good for you. The mark is there on Cain's forehead, clearly seen and written in clear unambiguous writing. But many cannot read the writing and are left wondering what the world is coming to.

They have seen what happened when one man, consumed by rage, jealousy, selfishness, and a desire to rule by any means necessary, murdered a quarter of the world's population. The shivering fear is, "What is going to happen in the world now that there are thousands who are actively laboring night and day to make the most heinous weapon of mass destruction ever known to man?" This is truly in keeping with the spirit of Cain. Can you see it? This one wants to rule by getting rid of or dominating the other. Why? Because he is running on the adrenaline of fear that the others might become more successful at winning, and he will then be enslaved by others who have superior weapons.

The truth is one way or another, they are both enslaved. Millions do not have enough to eat, yet governments are pouring billions into manufacturing, stockpiling these monstrous weapons of mass destructions. These weapons are not being made on order to make peace, as the governments would have you believe. Neither are they for defense and security, or for friendship and love. They are meant to terrorize through fear, hate, and jealousy, that they might cause through fear the subjugation or destruction of people's property and livelihood so that they may rule the world unchallenged. Yes, Cain lives on in his children through the inherited genes that they carry. Any report that he was seen recently should be comprehensibly dismissed; it's just one of his children who has displayed his genetic characteristics, and this mistake could be made quite easily. All his children have the same mark on their foreheads, but the mark has somewhat faded with the passing of time.

As more sophisticated weapons were invented, manufactured, and sold, so also has more blood been crying out from the ground, especially because most of these weapons of mass destruction can be used to murder from a distance, and death is meted out swiftly before most of the targeted victims have a chance to escape. There were twin attacks by a gunman who admitted that he planted a car bomb that exploded close to government offices, killing eight people. Then he drove to an island where a summer camp for the governing political party's youth wing was being held, and he murdered sixty-nine people, most of whom were teenagers. This man has been declared a paranoid schizophrenic after months of assessment, and he is likely to be detained in a mental institution rather than prison. In a multiple-page manifesto, he outlined his radical right-wing views and the steps he took in obtaining his powerful weapons. He also joined a club to increase his chances of obtaining a semiautomatic weapon six years later.

Even though the law prohibits the use of such dangerous weapons, many seek them. This man wrote, in his application for a license to own a semiautomatic weapon, that he needed the gun to hunt deer. I suppose that if Cain's father had asked him what he needed the knife for, he would have probably said, to hunt for goats. After the carnage that took place, the authority said that he wanted a tightening of the laws on semiautomatic weapons ownership. A committee has recommended a new law with greater emphasis on safety and preventative measures. These children of Cain and Seth are hell-bent on fighting each other, lying to each other, stealing from each other, spying on each other, killing each other, and hating each other.

At long last, however, they are realizing that things need to change. The only thing that I can see change is in speech, not their actions. They are still working frantically at subverting the actions of each other, still putting up barriers against any brother who does not fall in line with their own policies. They are still calling others to block a brother who lived under a different political regime. They are saying, "Let us use a trade embargo as means of forcing the hateful dissenter to submit and toe the line with a sanction so severe that even though we know that many people may die of hunger and diseases, it's okay because this one sees things differently from the others and does not follow orders, so they are being made to change." Things are changing so that even the big, mighty governments have no choice but to seek change. How?

I am very sure that you have seen the heads of governments or their diplomats franticly traversing land and having meetings with other governments and diplomats, discussing matters of not only national issues but international issues. What has caused these hives of activities? Because of the meltdown in the world's economy! These brothers have fought and killed each other, and it has become a way of life. But now a good reason to come together is the question they are now asking: how does one solve the seemingly impossible problems of not only their own individual national burden of debt but, just as important, the world? Instead of getting better, the debts are getting larger.

The mighty colonial powers that once poured scorn on their subjects are now turning to the what used to be derogatorily called "banana boat" economies, turning to them and seeking a light of hope for their economies. How the mighty have fallen! Those same "banana boat" economies are now being aggressively touted for business so that the once mighty colonizers may be saved from the abyss of a people's revolution against economic hell. These rescuers will soon need to be rescued themselves, but there will not be any with the ability to render help. They will look, but there will be none to help; they will look, but there will be none to save. They will all fall into the abyss of financial hell, because none of these governments is seeking a global solution. It's about "How can I swing the vote in my favor?" It's not "our," it's "my." Peace is talked at the table, but knives are being held behind their backs.

Cain did not see, or he could not have cared less about, the chaos that his action would have caused, and his children have made the same vain decisions. They have sown the bitter fruit of hate, and war is the result, with crimes of every description. Death, sorrow, and pain are the wages while hoping to reap the sweet fruits of peace, security, and plenty, with ruler-ship of the world being the ultimate goal of their endeavors. Yes, they fight and murder, hoping to have peace and security in the world. It never worked with their father, Cain, and it is painfully obvious that it is not working with his children. Killing each other with guns and dropping powerful Atomic bombs on the supposed enemy, who happens to be one's brother, has not worked and will never work. Their course of action will always have the total opposite of peace, but alas, his children have chosen to close their eyes to the fact that peace, and above all love, must first be in the hearts in order for it to be manifested and extended to the people of the world.

CHAPTER SIX

Imagine

Can you imagine sending your beautiful daughter and your lovely son off to school, waving to each other a last good-bye with pride and undying love welled up in your heart, your mind still fixed on the career paths that they might pursue, the loves they will encounter, and the loves of their lives?

But just as the scenario in the murder of Abel by Cain, the emotions of love, joy, and peace are shattered by one of your colleagues shouting out to you, "Have you heard the news? There has been a shooting at your school. Twenty-one are dead, and many are injured."

Stunned and in a panic, you drop everything and shout, "Where is my car?" Suddenly you cannot remember where you have parked your car, even though you have parked it at the same spot for many years. You are imagining the worst thing might have happened to your children, and you are out of your mind. You are shaking; fear is the demon that grips and controls your mind, and it won't let go. You shake nervously, and the car keys are in your hand, but you are still frantically searching for them. One of your colleagues tries to console you by telling you how she had a very similar experience, and everything worked out fine, but you cannot be consoled by some incident that happened years ago. You wish that you had the power to change time, because you would change it to just before your kids left for school this morning, when all was love and kisses and warm embraces. They would never have gone to school today.

On the way there, you begin to do something you have never done before, or at least you can't remember having done so. You pray out loud! Your boss is taken aback, turns to you, and says, "I did not know that you were Christian!"

You mumble with quivering lips, "I don't know what I am. I don't know if I am one. I don't even know what I've said, and I don't know if there is a God up there. But I've heard some people said that he is, and that he answers prayers. I've got nothing to lose. I'll call on him; maybe they are right."

You arrive at the school in about ten minutes, but it seems like it took a full hour. You shout to your boss, "Why are you driving so slowly?" You looked out the car window and realize that you are at the school. With barely enough strength left, you call out their names, but there is no answer. With a little more strength from somewhere, you call out again, but again there is no answer. The school is cordoned off by the police, and you are stopped from entering.

Hope springs eternal. They have a suspect who ended up shooting himself. Your children are safe; they were situated in the west wing of the school, but the shooting was in the east wing, so he did not get near them. It turned out that the young man who carried out this atrocity used to hang around with your son in the nearby park after school. You thought that he was a nice boy, but like Cain's mother, she doted on her son and thought he could do no wrong. When his father tried to correct his bad behavior, he was overruled by his mother; she wore the trousers in the house. She thought that her boy was the best in the world and that one of his teachers must have upset him, or else he would not have done such a thing. But when his room was searched by the police, they find automatic guns, high-powered rifles, hundreds of bullets, and even a couple of grenades. He'd acquired these items with the cognizance of the mother, who frequently cleaned his room.

Cain's children have found themselves with a great dilemma when even children are committing murders in schools, when children as young as nine are found with drugs for sale to their peers in school; that is a dilemma. But there is more to the problems found in schools, when a child misbehaves in school and is given some form of corrective discipline; if that child reaches home and complains to his parents, it's likely the teacher gets a visit from the parents with a barrage of verbal abuse, which sometimes transforms into physical abuse.

Let us take a look back at the relationship within Cain's family. His mother, Eve, loved her son so much that she could not see (or ignored) what she saw: what was needed was the training up of her child in the way he should go so that when he became mature, he would not turn aside from it and would follow in that good path. Yes, yes! The father did not act as the head of the family; he was satisfied to bury his head in the sand. He could not see what was happening in his own home, and when problems arose, he blamed everybody else but himself.

Cain and Abel's parents were living on a farm given to them by the benevolent authority, but they disobeyed the authority, and the contract was made void by their disobedience; they were summarily expelled from the paradise part of the farm. They were not living far from the farm and could still see the beauty and abundance that could have been theirs had they lived in obedience to the authority. The story of their expulsion from their former abode was relayed to the two sons, but Cain was very wrathful and angry that they were not now living in the peaceful, abundant surrounding. All that was asked of them now was that they make a little sacrifice and present the first unblemished fruits of their harvest to the authority.

Cain chose to ignore the request and presented unclean, blemished things from his harvest to the authority, which was a vengeful and despicable act against the authority. Cain was rebuked for his disobedience, arrogance, and disloyalty, and he was demoted from the ruler-ship that should have been his. His wrathful disposition prevented him from ruling, he was demoted, and his brother Abel was promoted. It seems that Cain went through a process of genetic modification.

It's very clear that all the problems of Cain and his children stem from the fact that his entire family was extremely dysfunctional. First, his mother acted as the head of the house, and his father lost his trousers. The authority always spoke to the father, and he in turn relayed the conditions, wishes, and desires of the estate owner, who was very loving and sympathetic to their needs; indeed, the authority supplied all their needs, and his laws were not grievous. They had a verbal contract with the estate owner, and although not written on tables of stones, it nonetheless must be obeyed. Someone once wrote, "Cease from anger and forsake wrath, so shall you dwell in the land and verily you shall be fed." This is exactly the opposite of what Cain did; he was full of anger and wrath, and through his anger and wrath, he murdered his brother, hoping to regain the ruler-ship that he'd lost through transgressions.

But his brother's blood was still dripping from his knife, and the earth was still crying out in shocked anguish at being choked by a dead man's blood. They were instructed by the owner of the estate, "This is the way that you should go. Walk in it, and you shall find peace, security, and rest to your life." Cain's anger and wrath blinded his vision of seeing the paradise in which he lived, and he was disqualified from the good that should have been his.

The children of Cain are in serious trouble. They have inherited their father's genes and are now plagued with diseases that not even their father had. Wherever Cain's children are found, you will encounter a number of diseases that were unheard of until recently. Diabetes is found everywhere and is a growing plague among both rich and poor alike, who seem incapable or unable to solve this problem even though the solution is readily available to those who want to be free from this plague. Heart disease, which often results in a large number of deaths, is a major concern. It has been found that these and many other medical conditions could be overcome by dietary means and regular exercise.

Added to these are global economic woes that are getting worse, because people are not taking heed to the wisdom of the authority, who knows the way and has given good advice through his wisdom. But scarcely is the wisdom of the authority being sought or heeded. Cain's children have become so clever and wise in their own wisdom—even though their wisdom has led them in the past in the wrong way and is leading them now in that way. The authority, who is the owner of the farm from which they were expelled, has given an open invitation to Cain's children: "Come buy gold (wisdom) without money and without price. A wise man will hear and increase in knowledge."

When Cain was expelled from his comfortable home, he recognized that he would be a vagabond and a fugitive on the earth—a wanderer. His children have not learned, and they have wandered into a global maze and cannot find the way out, even with all their wisdom and technology. They can build rockets on earth and launch them into the heavens, travelling at extraordinary speeds. Even though peace is called for and agreed to by the shaking of hands, the knife is still carried in the other hand. Their spies are given orders to see what the other is doing because there is no trust, and therefore the relationships are broken down because they were not built on trust or brotherly love. It is always "What's in it for me?" and is never "What's in it for both of us? How can we both benefit?" They all want to have ruler-ship, to dominate no matter how people protest to the contrary. Yes, the children of Cain and Seth have sent men to the moon, yet they cannot solve the problems they themselves have created.

Is there a way out for Cain and Seth's children, out of that bog into which they are sinking? Someone wrote a long time ago,

> Dear master; who has given us this bountiful farm for our benefit. We don't know the way in which we should go. We have come to realize that it is not in us to see beyond and thus direct our path to obtain the success for which we are seeking. Show us and teach us how to look after your farm as you have taught our grandparents long ago; whom you removed because of their not obeying your laws and breaking the covenant that you had with them. Instead, we have followed in the same disobedient way, and are reaping the bitter fruits of our waywardness we are still murdering, we are still killing, we are still robbing, we are still stealing, we are still corrupting others, we are still enslaving others, and now even the earth is

crying out because of the dead men's blood which
we made it swallow.

Now, even the earth is refusing to yield the abundance that
we once enjoyed. The rain, when it comes, arrives in anger
and rage, sweeping away all that is before it: houses, bridges,
animals, the food in the ground, and human lives. Massive
earthquakes trigger tsunamis, and great fires leave behind great
devastation. This was the cry of the ancients, when things went
awry and there seemed no way out of their troubles.

Cain and Seth's children face the same situations as those
ancients, but the ancients knew where, and to whom to turn for
help; they humbled themselves and turned to the owner of the
estate, who gave Adam and Eve clear instructions of how to live
safely and successfully, and who also taught their children. The
authority held nothing back from them. When they went astray
from his guidance and lost their way, they humbled themselves
and said, "Dear master, the authority, we have come to realize
that it is not in us to direct even our own paths: direct us on
how to live in it." The reply was,

"Wisdom cries without; with a clear voice she
speaks in the streets: She cries in the chief place

of concourse, in the openings of the gates: in the city she speaks her words, saying: How long, you simple ones, will you love simplicity? And the scorners delight in their scorning and hate knowledge? Turn at my reproof: look, I will make known unto you My wisdom which would guide you to the way of peace; But I have called, and you refused; I have stretched out my hand, and no man regarded it; But you have set at naught all my counsel, and would none of my reproof; but chose to follow your own knowledge and wisdom which will always lead death and destruction: The way that seems right in your eyes has only lead to darkness: but now the earth is rebelling against you. Desolation and destruction is coming as a whirlwind; distress and anguish is coming to you.

Then shall you call upon me, but I will not answer; you shall seek me early, but you shall not find me because I know how you hated my sound knowledge, and you have not chosen my fear: Your Authority! And you have set at naught all my counsel: you despised all my reproof. Therefore, you shall eat of the fruit of your own way, and be filled with your own devices. I have called to you and said, "Stand in the ways, and see, and ask for the old paths, where is the good way, and walk therein, and you shall find rest for your souls." But you said, we will not walk therein. The fear of me; The Authority, is the beginning of knowledge: but fools despise wisdom, "How long, simple ones, will you love simplicity? And scorners delight in their scorning, and fools hate knowledge? I have given you a holy good earth: but you have brought it to near desolation; but turn yourself around in sincerity of heart, and I will help you clear away the death dealing chemicals with which you have poisoned the earth.

Cain's problem was that he had no respect for the authority, who allowed him to live on the good earth through his benevolence. At least Cain realized his great mistake, because on his way out of his home, he said, "You are driving me out this day from home and family, and as a result I will become a vagabond and a fugitive in the earth." He became just that. But the horror of it all is instead of his children turning away from and forsaking the ways of their father, they have embraced his ways wholesale! And their grandparents looked on and sighed! This is the woman who had declared falsely, "I have gotten me a man from The Authority." This man, the first ever born to human beings, murdered his own brother.

Someone said in times past, "The heart of man is desperately wicked; who can know it! You cannot know it!" It is covered over with a thick layer of deceit, and what the eyes behold is a double agent with a knife to stab you in the back. The authority heard their cries in the past when they could not see their way out of their troubles, but no sooner had they received his help and things began to run smoothly again than they trusted in their own wisdom of selfishness and pride in the technology. The authority still loves and cares for these wayward children who inherited the genes of their father. The authority always responds to truth and sincerity from the heart. Only a meager few of Cain's children are willing to change, turn, and look after the authority's farm and estate the way he had instructed their grandparents, which they failed to do through disobedience. The authority has the antidote for corruption and the blood-soaked earth, and he promises to restore his farm as it was at the beginning.

It must be remembered that Cain's parents, Adam and Eve, were thrown of the original farm, which was situated on the east of the vast estate. They occupied an area just outside the perimeter, close enough for deep frustration to set in Cain's heart, which showed up in an attitude of, "I couldn't care less about the authority. You have thrown my parents out, and just because I have gotten rid of that usurper, my brother, you are throwing me out too. You are unfair, you are turning me out, and I shall become nothing more than a vagabond and a fugitive in the earth, away from family and the glory that is in the farm." It was because he murdered his brother and, in his arrogance, showed no respect for the authority that he was thrown out. His children should have learnt from his negative example; but sadly, the lessons have not been learnt. And why should they learn? With their wisdom, they can speak to each other from the nether part of the world with their technology. They can work magic, as it were, with their computers and all sorts of wizardry, so taking instruction from the estate owner is old-fashioned, is outdated, and makes no sense. Our wisdom is the way, they say, but the end will be calamitous.

The dark clouds are getting darker, gathering and thickening around the world right now. But if they could simply look to and take the advice of the authority, who is the expert on the times and seasons of when to sow and when to reap, what to weed out, and what to cultivate, then a worldwide Edenic scene would be generated with the guidance of the one who knows: the authority.

Sometime after Cain was thrown out of his abode and was well on his way to becoming a fugitive and vagabond, his mother gave birth to another son, whom she called Seth. She said, "This will replace Abel." Presumably she counted Cain as being dead because she did not make the mistake this time in saying, "I have gotten a man from the Authority." Once bitten, twice shy, as they say.

Cain's brother Seth was more in line with the authority's wishes; although not perfect, he taught his children the laws and wishes of the authority. This was indicated after one of his grandsons committed murder. After realizing that he had slipped into the way of Cain, the grandson repented and so was called Lamenta, for in anguish of heart for the sin he had done, he lamented; sorrow filled his heart, and he confessed to his wives. This was the first man in recorded history who had more than one wife; he was polygamous. The genes of Cain manifested in his behavior back then, but unlike Cain, some men came to realize that they were going in the wrong direction, and they turned to the laws and directives of the authority so that they might know how to live on their patch in harmony through the good wisdom and understanding of the estate owner, who knew what they should do, so that they may live in peace, love, and harmony with the earth, spreading his goodness throughout the entire world. They were and still are debtors—not to their fleshly minds to live after their understanding, but according to his wisdom; he weighed the actions that they took and knew whether the outcome would be good or bad. It was at this time that men began to call upon the authority.

But the whole earth became corrupted, and it grieved the authority that he let out his farm to these children. But to Seth, there was born a son called Enos. Seth noticed the violence, the mindless murders, and the general wickedness in the earth. He wanted nothing to do with that sort of lifestyle and way of living. He was grieved, and so was the authority, who saw that the wickedness was great in the earth and that every imagination of the thoughts of his tenants was only evil. Seth knew that such behavior would lead to the great anger of the estate owner because the farm that he'd let out to these children was corrupted and soaked in blood.

Men began to call upon the authority so that he might lead them back to the true way, guiding them in the right way to look after their farm, which would bring them true love and harmony with joy and peace in abundance. There were those who realized that they were debtors to the authority. And yes, they called, but only a tiny few heeded the advice given to them. It was much as it is now, because the very same conditions are in existence. They were the same attitudes recorded in the days of Noah. They mocked Noah and call him a fool because he heeded the authority's voice and built an ark on dry land, away from the sea and rivers. But Noah followed the instructions and built a vessel that would float on water. Whilst others perished in the water, Noah and his family were saved by it. The storm came, and then the gushing flood came. Only those who heeded the warning were saved.

Such would be the children of both Cain and Seth by the promise of the authority, if they follow the example of Noah, who realized that the corruption he saw was a sign that the authority would have to do something to rid the world of such blatant corruption, and the promise made to him by the authority that Noah and his children were to inherit the earth and should multiply and replenish the earth. The authority told him that not only the farm but the whole estate (the entire world) would be granted to them for an inheritance, where they would want for nothing in a life unending if they followed in obedience. The authority knew that they would be still be struggling with human weakness, frailties, and temptations, but he wanted them to give honor to the estate owner, by keeping their farm free from blood, theft, and hatred, and instead sought to lead others to his laws, commandments, and directives by doing their best and avoiding the errors that were manifested around them. Even though they themselves fell into the snares that the tempter had set for them, when they realized their failings and called to him in repentance with great sorrow of heart, he'd forgive them and right the wrongs that they had done.

The authority is so pleased with this new nation because of their willingness to turn from their wickedness, live by his loving laws and directives, and bring the first ripened fruits to him as a sacrifice. He has promised them that they would be able to live forever in a new, cleansed, and sanctified New Estate. The New World will be theirs forever, rent-free and in paradisiacal condition. Not only that, but he will sterilize and cleanse the whole earth of all evil and evildoers. Then shall the earth bring forth its increase in abundance. There won't be any concentrated chemicals that can poison the land; their food will be wholesome, pure, and life-giving. Even the leaves in the estate will be for the healing of the nation, as it was before Adam and Eve fell through disobedience. Yes, all things will be restored.

Adam and Eve, and then Cain, thought that they would be more successful and technical in choosing their own wisdom.

They thought that by doing so, they would be able to rule not only their own farm but the whole world, no matter what the authority had said. They knew that the authority is extremely wise in all his dealings. There is a way that seems right to men, but it usually turns out quite wrong. They came to realized that they were woefully wrong.

CHAPTER SEVEN

The authority send help

The authority was so concerned about the false and corrupt way of Cain and Seth's children that he appointed great men who, even though they had their fair share of human weaknesses and frailties, nonetheless tried to follow the principles laws and commandments that were given to them. Among these courageous men who stood up against the evils— the murders, the thievery, and downright debauchery who were running rampant in their society and the whole world—was a prophet called Abraham. He lived in their society, and he heard and saw that they made peace by killing their opponents, their brothers. Their peace came after much killing, and the conquered were made to sign away much of their independence. With a knife hanging over their heads, peace was secured by humiliating others, which naturally engendered a silent hatred toward the conqueror, who taught to his children and the next generation, and the next generation; it is carried on to successive generations into perpetuity. These children cared nothing about the good laws and benevolence of the authority, but Abraham had respect for his laws, his commandments, and his love. He saw that his father chose the ways of Cain, as did almost all of society. Abraham was so disgusted that he decided to pull up roots and move out of his familiar setting. That was when the authority was able to speak to him, and he showed Abraham his plans to rescue these children from committing corporate suicide.

Abraham was given a test to sacrifice his son to the authority so that he could test the limit of his loyalty, and how much and how far this man would go in obeying him. He passed that test successfully and was called a friend of the authority. Unlike Adam and Eve, who disobeyed the authority, or Cain, who was wrathful, arrogant, and disrespectful, he obeyed the authority, and it was counted to him for righteousness. Abraham had a son called Ishmael, by a servant girl, but this girl disrespected Abraham's wife, Sarah, because Sarah did not have a child. Sarah became pregnant and gave birth to a son called Isaac. In time, Isaac's wife gave birth to twins: Jacob and Esau. Rebecca; Isaac's wife loved Jacob, but Isaac loved Esau. This naturally caused a tug-of-war in the family and rendered it dysfunctional.

Isaac loved Esau because he ate and was very pleased of the venison that this son made for him' even Esau's clothes smelled of the field from which he caught and killed the meat that he prepared for his father, when Esau was away on his hunting expeditions, and his father Isaac's heart was made glad by the expectancy of enjoying his favorite meal cooked by his favorite son, who did it for the enjoyment of his father, who loved him.

Jacob, on the other hand, was loved by his mother, Rachel. He was a smooth and good-looking young man, but by the instigation of his mother, Esau was tricked out of his birthright. The result was Esau lost the birthright blessing that should have been his, to Jacob. Esau was tricked out of the birthright by the sleight of hand of both his mother, Rachel, and her favorite son, Jacob. Jacob married a cousin of his named Rebecca. There was born to Jacob twelve sons: Jacob's name was changed by the authority to Israel, and therefore his sons came to be known as the twelve tribes of Israel.

Before he was married, he contracted to Laban to work for him for seven years for the hand of Rachel in marriage, but he was tricked by Laban on the marriage night, and instead of Rachel, he slept with Leah, Rachel's sister instead. He did not realize it until the morning after he awoke. The custom was in that part, the older sister should (must) marry first, and therefore he had to work another seven years in order to marry the love of his life, Sarah. The tricked he played on his brother had now come back in another way to haunt him. To get back at Laban, his father-in-law, Jacob, negotiated a new contract with Laban that all the animals that were born plain would be Laban's, and all that were born ring-streaked or spotted would be his. Laban gladly agreed to this because there wouldn't be many cattle that would be born ring-streaked, but Jacob had a well-worked plan in place. He set up two sticks by the watering troughs so that when the cattle mated, they would look on the sticks, and the result was almost all the cattle were born ring-streaked, speckled, and spotted. This man was full of intrigues.

Nevertheless, it was through the lineage of this same Jacob that many great kings, prophets, and priests came, by the instigation of the authority, in an attempt to teach men the way of their estate owner, by giving them laws and commandments through these human agencies that would act as a guidepost in caring for his estate and their farms. Of those was a great man, a prophet called Moses, through whom laws and commandments were given by the authority to the people, who would guide and regulate their behavior that would eventually lead to peace and security. If they lived by those laws and commandments, they would enjoy the freedom not only of their farm but eventually the entire estate, the world. All that was asked of them was that they honor the wishes of the authority by keeping their farm free from blood and other pollutants that saturated the world.

But the children of Cain and Seth seemed incapable or unwilling to do his bidding and follow instructions coming from one of their flesh and blood. They were not always wayward children, however, because at times when troubles overtook them, and they realized their mistakes and remembered that the authority was very kind and compassionate to those who call on his help in sincerity. They called, and when he answered them, great rejoicing echoed in the air with great honor being showered on the authority who had delivered them. But after a few years, and sometimes after a few months elapsed, when the favor of the authority slipped from their memories; they would turn back to those same weak, beggarly elements that they loved! Where is the love?

In process of time, Moses died, and Aaron, Joshua, and others were raised up and tried to follow in the footsteps of Moses by directing the children of Cain and Seth in the path that they should go and honor the estate owner, the authority, who is the loving giver of their farm. "This is the way," he advised: walk therein, and you shall have peace in abundance with joy unspeakable, and you will have want for nothing.

But they answered, "Your way is too strict. We will do as our hearts dictates." The authority inspired a young man by the name of Samuel, who was loaned to the authority by his mother, who was a barren woman. She'd prayed with such intensity, that he who had the power to answer prayer would answer her prayer. She loaned him back to the giver because she knew that he would be always be her son.

This young man, who grew up in a place of worship, heard the call to service when he was a child, and he was content to serve as an assistant to the old priest Eli. He humbly served in the role that was given him, and did not seek to usurp the old man's position; though Eli was almost blind. He proved himself faithful and was used by the authority to anoint the man who would be king. The authority chose a man to be king whose attitude was in tune with his, yet the king himself inherited the weaknesses of his ancestors Adam and Eve, and Cain and Seth, so much so that he fell into the very same sin that he was condemning in others. But unlike Cain, who was arrogant and filled with pride and hate, he humbled himself when the prophet pointed out his fault, and he repented. That great king's name was David, a man after the authority's own heart.

David fell because he looked through his window one day and espied a beautiful woman having a bath. His emotions triggered a lust that very few men could control, so he pursued her, he loved her, and his love blossomed. But she was another man's wife! His sin was not only that she was another man's wife but that he had many young women from whom he could have chosen. He was called a friend of the authority because when his misdemeanor was pointed out to him, he humbled himself and repented. His reign was never surpassed by any king or leader of men, not even by his wise son Solomon, whose wisdom and great wealth was spread to distant lands; the Queen of Sheba travelled a great distance and brought gifts in abundance just to see the wealth of this king, and to hear for herself the wisdom that was told her. She was so overwhelmed by what she saw and heard that when she was ready to return, she exclaimed, "The half have not been told me."

Solomon had it all: wisdom, wealth, and power. Through all this wealth he became a magnet for women, and women were a magnet to him. Opposites attract, and with that attraction, his heart was led astray to worship strange gods. With all that knowledge, wisdom, and instruction given by his father David, the prophets who tended his courts, the law, his advisers, and the history of Adam and Eve, Cain and Seth, Abraham, Isaac, and Jacob (whether written down of by folklore), he had the wisdom of how he should walk so that he should avoid the sad fate of many, and he could follow in the footsteps of the few. But sadly, he too succumbed to the mighty gratifications of human nature. Nevertheless, he wrote much about how to be wise, following the wisdom of the wise, and the value of their instructions. There was a way that seemed right in the eyes of men, but the end usually turned out to be quite the opposite to what was intended. Taking good advice should have been the bedrock of his behavior, but with the attention and attraction of women, he proved to be weak as tow.

As a result of his turning away from the true path in which his father David walked, the kingdom's lineage was wrested from him and given to someone else. As usual, some walked in the way that the estate owner wished in their farm, but most did otherwise. Because they ignored the good advice of the authority, their land would not bring forth enough to sustain their families. The rain failed, they sowed against the cooperation of the land, they again spilled blood, and they acted contrary to what was for the good of nature. Therefore, they sowed much but reaped little, and the little that was produced could not satisfy their hunger.

Again, great prophets rose up to point that the wayward children of Cain and Seth were back to the path to good husbandry of the land, which would lead to the desired abundance and safety. The prophets guided them, and for a while they obeyed the prophets. They shouted out, "All that you say, we will do." They had no choice because they were in want, and indeed they followed the instructions and advice of the prophets—until prosperity was reestablished. Then after a year or two, or perhaps within a few months, they reverted back to trampling underfoot the word of the prophets who'd saved them.

Prominent among those prophets was Elijah. In his zeal, he put people to the sword in his bid to rid the land of those who he thought were leading the people astray, and at the same time he demonstrated his allegiance to the authority. The reigning king's wife, Jezebel, heard what the prophet had done to her prophets, and she got up in a rage and vowed to kill Elijah. Elijah heard of the oath taken against his life by this lady, and he fled far away and hid in a cave in the mountain. This was the man who'd stood up to and killed four hundred prophets, yet he ran away and hid in a cave because of the threat of a woman. He was a soldier in the authority's army, and he was on an assignment to bring back peace, but instead he ran away and hid in a cave.

Elijah had a very able student who took up the mantle. This young prophet was named Elisha. He followed Elijah where- ever he went, he saw and heard much, and afterward he took up the mantle of Elijah. After Elijah's passing, he acted just as Elijah had, but he kept his hands free from blood. He did not act according to his own will but followed the law of the authority, and the people obeyed his lead as they had his predecessor.

There were numerous priests and prophets after Elijah and Elisha, and many kings who reigned after David and Solomon. There has not been a king held in honor as high as David, there has not been a prophet who was held in such high honor after Elijah, and there has not been a priest held in such honor after Samuel. These men were not superhuman, and neither were they super-intelligent or super-anything, as their exploits might suggest. They were ordinary men who decided to honor the authority, and they tried to keep his laws and commandments by keeping their allotted farms in good condition, clearing out all the bad that they saw in themselves and encouraging others to do the same. They sought to avoid polluting their farm by spilling blood, and they maintained the standard of the good that their farm was capable of giving for their enjoyment and the honor of the estate owner, who had loaned them their farm without price.

But they had problems with the people with whom they interacted: the people were never satisfied with the fat of the land, and they were never satisfied with the instructions that their leaders provided. From time to time, they rebelled and demanded what they were not capable or worthy of: some wanted to rule but were unqualified; some wanted to act as priests but only wanted to be held in honor of men, appointing to themselves as priests who were corrupt (contrary to the will of the authority). They were met with much disappointment and even death.

The children of Cain and Seth were very difficult to deal with, yet from time to time, there arose some from lowly backgrounds who were made kings, prophets, or priests by the authority, whose wisdom and knowledge was unmatched by the experience that he had accumulated. He judged the hearts of Cain and Seth's children, and they were not judged by their physical stature, their family's backgrounds, their education, or their wealth. He judged the hearts and intents. David, the greatest king, was a lowly shepherd boy, and he was chosen and elected to rule as king over a nation with twelve tribes whose tendency was to act contrarily to what was desired of them. Moses went up to a mountain to receive the contract from the authority: laws to help regulate their lives and bring peace and harmony to their farms. He stayed a while on the mountain, and when he arrived back in the camp, he found that the people had built to themselves a molten calf, which they were worshiping and frolicking around naked; they'd engaged in other ungodly behaviors too. Moses was incensed, and in a rage he threw down the tablets of the laws and broke them to bits.

A long time ago, it was written, "And GOD saw that the wickedness of man was great in the earth and that every imagination of the thoughts of his heart was only evil continually." The programs that these children of Cain and his brother Seth watched as entertainment were very revealing. The most watched and enjoyed were those that were filled with violence of every genre—people getting killed by a host of different methods. The knife was still a very potent weapon and was used by many. It could be easily concealed about the person and flicked from a pocket or sheath, and it could be worn about the body with deadly consequence. It was the weapon used by Cain, the wan who'd murdered a quarter of the world's population.

But through the race to invent more advanced methods for killing each other, they progressed and invented a weapon called a gun. With that weapon, personal contact was no longer necessary. Killers could be quite a long distance away from their target, and they used that weapon to kill their brothers. The shot was fired, and the brother fell dead.

CHAPTER EIGHT

Entertainments

People are influenced to a large degree by the entertainment that is enjoyed by the masses. When a person watches a violent movie, his emotions become involved. If the hero hits or kills the criminal, the emotions of the viewer empathize with the hero and give mental assent, cheering him on in whatever activity he does—theft, physical assault, murder, illicit sex, and more. Movies and television are two of the mind-numbing entertainment channels that are effective devices to entice and corrupt the children of Cain and Seth to go astray; they have become the beautiful tree with the forbidden fruit in Cain and Seth's garden. People ate and became filled with its beautiful, sweet fruit; being filled, they became intoxicated; being intoxicated, they knew not that they were psychologically drunk.

The human mind was where the battle began. The thoughts of the children of Cain and Seth were influenced by their emotions, which then formed their characters. Their characters could be summarized in an old proverb: "As a man thinks in his heart, so is he." They became what they thought about all day long, and their thoughts were tragically only evil. As a result of their thinking, they wandered into a place where they became disorientated and lost. In a state of drunkenness, they started to call darkness light, and light was darkness. Their leaders became the blind leading the blind, and when that happens, as one king said, they would both fall into the ditch.

Cain and Seth's children need not fall into the ditch, because the estate owner who gave them a part of his estate knows every inch of their farm, and he knows what is good for the well-being of the farm and them. All they needed to do was quite simple: call for help, and ask the estate owner the way out of the ditch into which they have fallen. The way was clearly marked and visible, with a bright shining light to guide anyone to safety. But they were drunken by the spirit of their own corrupted minds, dulled by their inventions, intoxicated by their mind-numbing entertainments, and disorientated by the darkness, which they thought to be light. And so the children of Cain and Seth lived in peril, and are more so now. Even the earth refuses to soak up the rain that falls on it, fires destroy hundreds of acres of vegetation and houses, and monetary and financial institutions are in a state of total collapse. "Perilous times hard to deal with" have caught up with the children of Cain and Seth. The authority has been calling out to these children, "This is the right way that I'm showing you, walk in it, and the peace and security that you seek, the abundance, the success in all your dealings will be obtained."

But these children, drunken by their mind-numbing entertainments and blinded by their electronic inventions, stiffened their necks in their pride and shouted back to the authority, "We will not walk therein."

The leaders of the people led the people astray by making them believe in their false hopes of a brighter future, knowing full well that the bright future promised was but a pipe dream. Some of the children were waking up out of their dark night of slumber ever so slowly, realizing that something was not at right with what they were being told by their leaders. In fact, something was very wrong with their world: the sun, moon, stars, and human leaders were not giving light—they were not shining. The light that they were seeing was darkness, and the leaders were nothing more than false prophets, hypnotizing the people with their well-rehearsed, bleached-out platitudes, which had lulled the people into a false sense of safety.

The darkness experienced by the world of these children of Cain and Seth, could be demonstrated by an example. One nation was in union with some others. The government called for a referendum to ascertain from his cabinet and the general public whether they should stay in or exit from this union in which they were a very important member. It transpired that members of the government's own cabinet were split: some opposed their own prime minister, who was very firm in his belief that they should stay in this union because of the advantages of trade with such a large market, and he reasoned that all those trading advantages could be lost by separating from this union. The cabinet members in his own government who opposed this union also opposed their own leader; they reasoned that the country could stand on its own, outside of this union, by obtaining trade from the bigger world and by taking back their own country from the union-imposed laws that each member in the union must obey. The opposers of this union felt that this robbed their country of the ability to independently make laws. It was a question of sovereignty, independence, and self-determination. They would take back control of their borders, immigration would be controlled, and the contribution that was spent being in the union would instead be spent on hospitals, schools, and other necessary things.

With all the discussions and debates by the parties, the people became confused and disorientated as to which way they should vote. The ruling party was split in two, and the prime minister said, "We must stay in the union." Part of his cabinet opposed him. Curiously, opposition parties, who would normally be drawing swords against whatever the government said, joined with the prime minister in staying in. Those who were in favor of coming out of the union, ministers of the cabinet from the government's side, were in effect being an opposition party within their own party, running against their own prime minister. They were joined by a few members from the opposition parties who vehemently opposed staying in this union.

One writer said, "Darkness covers the earth: and Gross Darkness covers the people." The ruling government being split by opposing views by cabinet ministers from within equaled darkness. The people observing the confusion from within the government by cabinet ministers blowing hot and cold from the same governmental cistern equaled gross darkness and confusion that covered the people. They couldn't see and knew not which way to go, because the darkness was such that a man could feel it "like the darkness of Egypt." The people went to the polling stations and voted, still in darkness. As a result of the darkness, the majority voted to leave the union, and no sooner had the decision been made to leave than within a week, some people began to see a little light. A call was made for there to be another referendum. The political leaders who were in darkness and confusion could not lead the people to the promised land flowing with milk and honey.

With all the debating, discussions, and arguments, there was not one single voice heard, and not a prayer made in appealing to the authority for his help—even though he was the one who gave them a part of his estate in which there was gold and diamonds that could be safely mined. The earth had become contaminated with blood and was cursed as a result of Adam's disobedience, but the authority is the light, and he is still willing and able to lead them in the right way to decontaminate the land and cause it to flourish and produce an abundance, because he knows the land inside out, and because he loves the children of Cain and Seth. All he asks of them is that they should ask, and it shall be given them. Knock, and it shall be opened unto them. Seek, and they shall find even more than they seek. He only asks that they come to him as a loving father, and he will "supply all their needs according to his riches of wisdom and knowledge that he possess." He will teach them the right way to produce verdant greenery to behold, as well as pure fresh breeze with birds singing in melodious strains as they fly pass on their ways.

But like Cain, these children would rather accuse each other of their mistakes and arrogance, instead of seeking the real truth to discover why things have turned out the way they have. They seek wrong instead of right, darkness instead of light, dysfunctional leadership instead of good examples, hate instead of love. The children of Cain and Seth would then realize that they had become lost and need to know the way—but how could they know except for someone who knows the way to teach them, guiding them in the right way? Instead of looking to the estate owner, who knew the right way, they ignored him. Instead of trusting in him, they worshipped their false gods of money and military might, seeking peace by inventing and manufacturing weapons of mass destruction! The children go wandering like lost sheep without a shepherd, because they still trusted in their own wisdom and strength. Their leaders have lied to them for political advantage, for the accumulation of wealth, and for ruler-ship of the world, be that at a local level or an international level.

Adam and Eve, the parents of Cain and Seth, made a grave mistake, and as a result they were thrown out of the farm that was prepared for them. They were told what to do, and the consequence of not following the good advice of the authority was losing their beautiful farm, which was stocked with all that was needed for them to live a joyous and fulfilling life. If they wanted more adventurous pursuits, there were mountains of various heights, and they could go diving in the rivers, lakes, and the sea. They could call the lions, bears, and other animals and play with them, because the one who created the farm made sure that everything in that farm was very good; there was no aggression in either animals or humans, and there was nothing to fear. Adam was given good advice by the estate owner: "Don't touch the fruit that I told you of, neither should you eat of it, or you would die." That was a test for Adam to see whether he would be obedient and loyal to the estate owner, and whether he would choose his own way, which would in effect mean rebellion against the benefactor.

One day whilst Adam was tending to his garden, a sweet charmer came to Eve and sweet-talked her into eating the fruit that was forbidden. She seduced her husband to eat it too. Eve was led away by her emotions, and Adam became weak by the persuasive voice and charm of his wife; he lost his head and by default rejected the estate owner's advice, as well as rejecting all that was given him and his wife in preference to their right to choose for themselves their path regarding what was right in their own eyes. They had their referendum.

The path that Adam and Eve chose led to the first man ever born to human beings, Cain, murdering his own brother, Abel. It was a case of rulership of the world by any means necessary. Adam was in the position of being the ruler of the world, and he lost it by disobedience. Adam lost it, and so Cain was the natural successor in line for that position, but he lost it because of his arrogance and by dishonoring the estate owner. Cain's problem was that he was spoilt by his mother, who thought that she had gotten a man child from the Lord. The family was so dysfunctional, so out of tune with reality, and so lost that they could not even make right decisions. The path that Adam and Eve took led to their being expelled from their Garden of Eden, losing the peace that they once enjoyed, and losing the relationship with their master, the authority, who gave them the freedom of their world. They lost the sweet communion that they had with him, as well as the relationship that they had with the animals.

Most of the animals' attitude toward them changed; they became fiercely aggressive toward them, and some would even try to kill them for food. When the farm was given to them, there was no blood spilled on that pristine earth, no sorrow of heart, and no crying with grief. But now the earth was forced to open its mouth and drink in the blood of the dead, and the blood cried out to the authority who heard the cries of victims suffering by the hand of their brothers, who in their arrogance, selfishness, pride, and hardness of heart shouted out to the authority, "I don't care about anyone else: Am I my brother's keeper?" After being asked by the authority to explain the noise of his brother's blood echoing from the ground, it is the sound that peaks, saying, "My brother has just murdered me with a knife. Please avenge my blood on my murderer, who has taken my life away from me." The animals also smelt the blood and heard the voice of that righteous man shouting from the now contaminated and corrupted earth, and in an attempt to avenge their faithful and true friend's blood, some of them became wild and ran away from man, fearful that they might become victims. Others became violently aggressive toward him. That was the price that Adam and Eve paid: they were the first people who witnessed the first funeral in the world, and they were the first to suffer grief over the death of a loved one.

Cain was shocked into reality when he was told that he was to be banished from his community and his family. He cried, "This punishment is too hard for me," indicating that he believed that the authority was unfair. After all, he only killed his brother Abel so that he could not ascend to the throne. Cain was banished from his comfort zone and became the first man to roam the world as a fugitive and vagabond. "When you till the ground, it shall not now yield her full strength as before," he was told by the authority. In an attempt to save the world from being totally corrupted by the children of Cain and Seth, the authority sought him out as a man who was sick to the heart of all the drunkenness, the murders, the rapes, the incest, the thefts, and all other crimes. He said to the man whom he found, whose name was Noah, "Build me an Arc that I might save you; for only you have I seen righteous with an upright heart in all the earth. Bring also all other species that are on the face of the earth." The authority said that the antediluvian world was corrupt to the core, and he would establish a new world through Noah and his family.

CHAPTER NINE

Passing of the Genes

B ut they were the inheritors of the genes of Adam and Eve, as were Cain and Seth. The deluge took away the world of the corruption and practices of sinners, but it could not wash away the blood that had been swallowed up by the earth. Everything continued in a way of conformity to the laws and commandments of the authority: there was peace and harmony with all creation until one of Noah's great-grandchildren, a man called Nimrod, who was a leader in his community. He was aware of the flood and the fact that only eight persons of the world, his family, were saved as a result of Noah taking heed of the laws and commandments of the authority. The authority's wish was that the earth be replenished, populated by peaceful, loving, and kind people who would respect the giver of their farm, and who would populate the whole world with a lifestyle that would reflect and honor the authority.

Nimrod had other ideas. Nimrod thought that he could outsmart the authority by building a structure so large and so high that if there was another flood, it would never be high enough for anyone in that building to be lost. It would reach up to the heaven, and no one would be lost in such a deluge. Nimrod was a mighty hunter in the world. It was thought that his skill in hunting was not limited to hunting wild animals for food, but also for sporting activities as well. Because of his prowess, he became the commander in chief of his army and also of his community, of his world. With such great position, he became the undisputed leader of the people—what he said went. But his hunting powers led him to hunting men if they refused to follow in his army; if they ran away and hid, he would soon track them down and put them to the sword. There was not another to compare in his class as a hunter or military leader.

Nimrod's first kingdom was called Babel, but it is more commonly known by the name of Babylon. Babylon was the chief city for the worship of many gods and strange beliefs. It was also a city where anything went, especially in regards to sexual perversions. The people were of one mind in the building of the tower, and because they spoke the same language, nothing that they thought of was too difficult. But this was in direct disobedience and opposition to the wishes of the authority, who had encouraged them to "multiply and subdue the earth." They said, "Let us build us a city and a tower, whose top may reach unto heaven; and let us make us a name, lest we be scattered abroad upon the face of the whole earth." It is said "rebellion is as the sin of witchcraft," and bear in mind that this was a city with all sorts occult practices. But when the authority looked and saw the beginning of their structure, and he knew that it was not only disobedience but open rebellion against his will, he sent angels with great abilities, and they changed the tongues of the people so that they could not carry on the building of the tower. As a result, the people dispersed themselves to the four corners of the world, and they were forced to obey the will of the authority.

As the people spread abroad, they could not speak in the same language as before, but they carried on worshipping the strange gods and idols. The gods and idols became variations of those that were worshipped before the dispersion. The people also carried on the sexual perversions as before, as was said in the antediluvian times by the authority: "Every imagination of man's heart, was only evil continually." Every generation that followed Adam and Eve, Cain and Seth, and Noah and Nimrod has experienced the degenerated depravities of the human species: blood cry unto blood; each generation has experienced blood being spilled as never before. There was also sexual slavery, especially of the very young, and the poorer nations were duped by the corrupters of wealthier nations, pretending to be tourists and seeking opportunities to help them out of their miseries—while in reality enslaving them for their own debauched self-gratification. Where ever you go, you would hear the same disbelief expressed among the older people: "It was never like this when we were young! What is the world coming to?" It seems that everyone wants to kill someone else, without any sense or good reason. Through education and science, the world has come to learn that people can acquire the ability to speak languages other than their own native tongues.

This became necessary for dealing in trade and commerce, as well as other joint ventures for the supposedly mutual benefit of the parties. But as was noted before, everyone seeks his own advantage over the other; each one usually has a knife behind his back, so to speak, even if it is no more than a commercial or financial knife. I hope that you realized this was the very same way that Cain murdered his brother. They were talking amicably, or so it seemed to Abel, and they were out in the field when Cain produced a knife, "his weapon of mass destruction," and slew his brother. But the blood spoke clearly from the ground, and the authority heard the words that were being spoken in a distinct voice that only he could understand. The voice of the blood was calling for revenge on the person who had cause his death by wasting his life blood on the ground, which was forced to drink it down into its system. It was the one thing that it was not designed to drink; it was foreign and spoke of death. The earth, the ground, was designed to sustain and produce life.

CHAPTER TEN

What they could not see

It is hard to imagine that Adam, Eve, and Cain could have possibly seen the devastating traumas that would result in deaths, sicknesses, crimes, wars, murders, mental health, and psychological problems that would plague the entire world, depriving it of the peace that should have been its legacy. How could they? They could not have seen a beautiful young English politician lady who was a beacon of hope to her country and the world, who gave her life in helping her neighborhood, whose neighbor was the whole world. She was gunned down and knifed to death right there in her own community, in cold blood. But like Abel's blood, her blood speaks to the world by saying, "My blood was spilled because I loved to help my fellow man. Yes, it's because of my death that I am now known to the world for my love to them, and for the sacrifice that I have made to show you what was in my heart."

No, they could not have known that a man would walked into a nightclub in France and shoot to death forty-nine people in cold blood, and he would have slaughtered even more had it not been for the intervention of the police officers. No, they could not have seen that over thirty people in France were gunned down for whatever reason. No, no, no! They could not have seen the number of innocent children gunned down in cold blood in their classrooms in many parts of the world. No, they could not have possibly witnessed the agony of those parents who, just a short while ago, had waved good-bye and blew kisses to their loved ones, their joys. No, it's not possible that they could have seen the scourge of HIV, a scourge that touched almost every area of the world, and there is no cure for the sufferers. No, it is not possible that they could have envisaged the turmoil of the Arab spring, the slaughter that took place in Iraq—a conflict to which there seemed to be no ending but that has spread fear in virtually every country in that area. No, No, No! They could not have seen the misery by the warring factions in Syria that witness hordes of people fleeing from their towns and cities. They have no homes, because their homes have been demolished and flattened by bombs and bullets, and the many lives that have been lost in the sea, fleeing in flimsy, unseaworthy, and overcrowded vessels operated by men whose only interests are financial gains—and their gains are at the expense of poor refugees. No, they could not have seen the little children gasping and struggling to breathe to take in their last breaths in the cold water, their mothers and fathers being helpless themselves as they drown together!

With the ever-increasing mountain of complexities in the world, with no permanent solution in sight, the world stands in peril because the rulers of the nations are forever fighting to rule the world so that they could manipulate situations to their national advantage and crush others who might not be part of their favorite clan. Ruler-ship of the world by Cain and Seth's children could never be the solution that plagues the world, and the why is quite simple: the person would need to have love that transcends: race, color, and ethnic diversity—true love! Yes, love. True love would rule in the heart and would be the one and only principle that would be manifested in his actions, not just talk. He would naturally lead the children of Cain and Seth to the laws and commandments of the authority, the path that would lead them back to the Eden of abundance of peace, joy, and love without rancor. A great part of the problems in leadership with the children of Cain and Seth is the love of money. A long time ago, a well-known apostle once wrote, "For the love of money is the root of all evil." It is so loved because money can buy anything, including men. In their world, money bought the services of men of every sort that includes the hiring of spies who would report on anyone who is not favored by the leader, and people would be shut out of the community for the slightest misdemeanor, or maybe even be murdered.

History is full of men who set out to lead the people into a utopian world, raising their standard of living, freedom, peace, and security. But a little farther along their journeys, the bubble always bursts. To be fair, some meant what they said, and was trying hard to achieve the promised outcome, but they were derailed by circumstances beyond their control: the financial markets slumped, the value of their currencies was devalued, there were national strikes, and that promised venture that was being pursued was forced to surrender to forces outside their control. Many men have sought to lead the world by the strength of their military forces, but might does not necessary means right. Might is right equates to dictatorship and bullying by whatever name is given to the system (communism, democracy, or whatever). Cain wanted to rule by his military might, a knife, but his plan ran into a problem that he had never thought of: he did not realize that his brother's blood had a voice that could speak, and it told the story of his murder.

If governments with their military generals had seen in their minds eye the millions of soldiers and civilians that would be killed and maimed, and those left destitute by rash decisions, would they have gone to war? Would they have destroyed those buildings and other monuments that took years of planning and construction? If you take a look through the pages of history, you would notice that those wars were started by governments and their generals who were starry-eyed with their hopes of military conquests and successes, with their governments ruling and subjugating the world, turning people into nothing more than common slaves. They convened their cabinets of old men and decided to go to war, calling on young men to put their young lives on the line at the behest of their governments and the military generals. But when conflict came to an end, those young men, who had aged as a result of their wearied and perilous battles, were usually seen walking the streets with no money or shelter, trusting on charities for help. Those generals were decorated with military medals for their "victorious" wars.

All these military activities by the governments seem to have no human plan or solution in sight. The solutions need to bring about desires that all humans have longed for: peace and security, joy in the soul, prosperity with no fighting for leadership of the world, and no blood on the ground. All these things were given to Adam and Eve with the good favor of the authority, free and without cost, but they lost them because of disobedience. "Touch not, and neither eat of the thing that is forbidden, lest you die." Adam must have given the same instruction that he had received from the authority to Eve. She must have had the same glorious promises of eternal life in the paradise farm in which they lived. "Simply follow the good shepherd, who will lead you into green pastures flowing with milk and honey."

But there was a slippery, slimy serpent who opposed the authority and set about undermining his authority by turning them away from the right path that would have led them to green pastures. That serpent deceived the woman who was called Eve; she was called Eve because she was deceived by the smooth-talking, good-looking serpent, and in so doing they lost the fullness of all that they had! Men have been trying since then to obtain what they have lost, but they are forever going in the wrong direction, travelling on the wrong path. One prophet said to some of his loyal followers, "Broad is the road that leads to destruction, and many there be that go in there-at, but, because Narrow is the way that lead to life; and Few there be that enter there-at." Since the fall of Adam and Eve, men have been following the broad road. Either they don't know, or because of their arrogance and puffed-up technological minds, they do not want to know.

CHAPTER ELEVEN

The hope

B ut there is a voice that comes shouting over the restless waves of humanity: "I Am the way, the truth, and the light, and if you follow in my way, in my laws; you will not walk in darkness, You are walking without My light, but a day is coming, it is a day of darkness and of gloominess, a day of clouds and of thick darkness; but those who come to me for life will find it, if they come to me for light, they will find it: for I am the Light sent from The Authority." But first you, the children of Cain and Seth, must "beat your swords into ploughshares and your spears into pruning-hooks," and then you shall achieve the desire of all nations: peace. For then nation shall not lift up a sword; or a knife against nation; neither would they learn war anymore. Then your land will be cleansed and purified not by your chemicals that poison the earth in your attempt to make it productive, but by the authority. The love and patience that is now being shown to the children of Cain and Seth by the authority testifies that he is still calling them to come to him so that they would find what they were always looking for: peace with security in an atmosphere of love being shed abroad in the hearts when obedience to the authority's laws and commandments are adhered to.

The authority has promised that when the children have made the turn, then their land will be cleansed and purified, as at the first. Their farm will flourish and bring forth in abundance. When it rains, it will not cause floods; when the winds blow, there will be no need for them to be fearful that it will bring a destructive force. He will have pacified the rage and convulsions of the earth, because he would have purged the belly of the earth of the blood that it was made to swallow, as well as the chemicals that made the children of Cain and Seth sick with death, dealing with cancers, diabetes, and burgeoning waistlines that result in sickness and diseases that are pandemic in the earth.

And what about ruling the world as an ambition? The ravenous sting of that desire would be negated because everyone would be able to sit under his own tree, feed off his own vine, and drink from his own well—all offering up good, pleasant gifts and sacrifices to the benevolent giver of his farm, the authority. Yes, Cain murdered Abel, his own flesh and blood, because his brother honored the authority and had respect for him. He showed this by offering him the best of what he had: the first fruit of his abundance. Cain, on the other hand, had neither honor nor respect for the benevolent giver of the farm, the authority, who transferred the ruler-ship of the world to Abel. For this, Abel was murdered, and for this, Cain lost the very thing that he was seeking to regain: ruler-ship of the world. But Cain could not obtain it, because the right to rule the world was transferred to another who had proven and submitted himself in humility and love to the authority. He loved the authority so much that he was willing to give up his own life to save the children of Cain and Seth, and this he did in honor, praise, and glory to the authority. This person obeyed the voice of the authority, walking in his laws and commandments to the fullest extent that the authority said of him, "This is My beloved Son in Whom I Am well pleased," and thus he was honored by the authority, who has also given him a name that is above every other name that is named, whether in heaven, on the earth, or under the earth.

This would have been the legacy and the inheritance of Adam—had he not disobeyed the advice of the authority. This was also the grand prize that would have been handed down to Cain had he not shed the innocent blood of his righteous brother

Abel, who offered up to the authority a gift and sacrifice of a sweet-smelling savor, because his heart was set in accordance to the law of love; that love sought out the things that are pleasing to the authority and others, love that is kind and seeks to please not its own self but the things that make for the joy or betterment of others. "It is always others before me, the self." Had Cain done the same, the scepter would have been his. One sage wrote, "Cease from anger and forsake wrath." Those were the very things that caused Cain to murder Abel. The children of both Cain and Seth are suffering under heavy burdens of woes and pain, along with the whole world that is waiting for the redemption that was offered. At the moment, they are all groaning, but the one who made that promise does not lie; neither does he slumber nor sleep. So tell those children of Cain and Seth, "Be patient and wait; he is working out his timely plan and preparing the ground for the day when you, the children, shall be restored to your paradise of Eden's green and pleasant land, and God himself will wipe away all tears from your eyes."

The Beaming Light

The king of glory came to reign
Into a darkened world of shame.

His brightness dimmed the very sun,

Yet few gave him glory and bless his name.

Away with him! they shouted loudly.

To reign over us—this cannot be.

A peasant in a stable born?

This cannot be the son of God.

Darkness covered the very earth—

And gross darkness the people.

The redeemer of humankind, he's called.

Yes, he came to save his own people.

He's coming back to earth some sweet day,

Clothed with a cloud, his glory beaming.

Few can see that it's now happening.

Only those who look will see his appearing.

The trumpet sounds: lo, he's coming.

The wise ones a-rise, their lamps brightly burning.

Get dressed to meet the king; he is coming.

The table is spread; now it's time for the feasting.

You have suffered with me; now you'll reign
with me.
You have denied yourself to follow me.
You were mocked and despised by a cruel world.
Now, enter into the joy of your Lord.

On my right-hand sit, I hear him beckon.
All things are ready for the bride of the Lamb.
Clothed all in white with garments gleaming,
He smiled with his eyes, his glory beaming.

Then shall the voice of weeping be no longer heard in all my estate, or the voice of crying. There shall be no more thence an infant of days, nor an old man that hath not filled his days, for the child shall die a hundred years old. And they shall build houses and inhabit them, for there will be no enemy to conquer them. They shall plant vineyards, eat the fruit, and be satisfied. They shall not build and then have to flee because of the destruction of their homes, or because of genocide by evil men, or because of bullets and bombs that spill the blood of infants. My people "shall inherit the earth, and shall delight themselves in the abundance of peace; for the wicked will be cast out of it," and mine elect shall long enjoy the work of their hands. They shall not labor in vain, or bring forth for trouble, for they are the seed of the blessed, the redeemed of the Lord, and they shall bring forth their offering: a sweet-smelling savor well pleasing to the authority, the Lord, and their offspring with them.

And it shall come to pass that before they call, I will answer, and while they are yet speaking, I will hear. The wolf and the lamb shall feed together, and the lion shall eat straw like the bullock, and dust shall be the serpent's meat. "They shall not hurt or destroy in my holy mountain," sayeth the authority, the Lord. The children of Cain and Seth, and all creation, will have what they have been crying for since Adam and Eve fell, and what was turned out of Eden: peace and security unending.

The End